CORE LANGUAGE SKILLS

Similes and Metaphors

Kara Murray

PowerKiDS
press

New York

Published in 2015 by The Rosen Publishing Group, Inc.
29 East 21st Street, New York, NY 10010

First Edition

Editor: Sarah Machajewski
Book Design: Jonathan J. D'Rozario

Photo Credits: Cover Blend Images - JGI/Jamie Grill/Brand X Pictures/Getty Images; p. 5 AntonioDiaz/ Shutterstock.com; p. 6 urciser/Shutterstock.com; p. 7 (hotel) anshar/Shutterstock.com; p. 7 (palace) Neil Mitchell/Shutterstock.com; p. 8 Sergey Novikov/Shutterstock.com; p. 9 (porcupine) l i g h t p o e t/ Shutterstock.com; p. 9 (dog) Olga Taranik/Shutterstock.com; p. 10 Steve Byland/Shutterstock.com; p. 11 Pichugin Dmitry/Shutterstock.com; p. 15 BMJ/Shutterstock.com; p. 16 limpido/Shutterstock.com; p. 17 altanaka/Shutterstock.com; p. 18 Stocksnapper/Shutterstock.com; p. 19 Nicholas Prior/The Image Bank/Getty Images; p. 21 Zurijeta/Shutterstock.com.

Library of Congress Cataloging-in-Publication Data

Murray, Kara.
Similes and metaphors / by Kara Murray.
p. cm. — (Core language skills)
Includes index.
ISBN 978-1-4777-7353-6 (pbk.)
ISBN 978-1-4777-7354-3 (6-pack)
ISBN 978-1-4777-7352-9 (library binding)
1. Simile — Juvenile literature. 2. Metaphor — Juvenile literature. 3. Figures of speech — Juvenile literature.
I. Murray, Kara. II. Title.
PE1445.S5 M87 2015
428.1—d23

Manufactured in the United States of America

CPSIA Compliance Information: Batch #CW15PK: For Further Information contact Rosen Publishing, New York, New York at 1-800-237-9932

CONTENTS

WHAT ARE SIMILES AND METAPHORS?

Think about the last book you read. Did the words create pictures in your mind? The author may have used **similes** or **metaphors** to do this. Similes and metaphors help a writer **compare** two things. They **describe** something by comparing it to something else.

Similes and metaphors are a lot alike, but there's one important difference. Similes use "like" or "as," and metaphors don't. However, you can use both to make your writing fuller and richer. Read on to learn more about them.

Figure It Out

What's the difference between a simile and a metaphor?

Find the answer to this question and the others in this book on page 22.

Using similes and metaphors is a great way to improve your writing.

MAKING COMPARISONS

Writers use similes and metaphors to help us understand what they're writing about. They use one thing to help us understand something else.

Let's look at some examples. The sentence "This water is as cold as ice" compares how cold the water is to how cold ice is. Since ice is very cold, we know the water must be very cold, too.

This simile gave our sentence more power. Do you think it's more interesting than simply saying "The water is cold"?

hotel

Figure It Out

The sentence "This hotel is a palace" is a metaphor. What does the comparison tell us about the hotel? Why?

palace

7

COMPARING LIKE THINGS

Similes and metaphors work when the things being compared have something in common. Suppose you want to talk about an animal whose fur is "as smooth as silk." What animal fits here, a porcupine or a dog?

First, think of what silk is like. It's shiny, soft, and smooth. Next, think of a porcupine. It's not shiny. It's not soft. It's not smooth, either! You can't compare it to silk. Now think of a dog. If its fur is shiny, soft, and smooth, you *definitely* can compare it to silk!

Figure It Out

Does the simile "My brother is as happy as a dragon" make sense? Why or why not?

SILK

silk shiny smooth soft	porcupine	dog
		✓
		✓
		✓

LEARNING SOMETHING NEW

Similes and metaphors work when readers are familiar with both things being compared. But they also work when readers only know one of the things. A simile or metaphor can help readers learn something new.

What do the painted bunting and a rainbow have in common? Does it make sense to use a metaphor to compare them?

Look at the sentence "A bird called the painted bunting wears the colors of the rainbow." The painted bunting doesn't *actually* wear a rainbow. However, if a reader can imagine what a rainbow looks like, they can imagine how colorful the painted bunting is. This metaphor could help readers who have never seen this bird understand the point you're trying to make.

Figure It Out

The sentence "David is as strong as an ox" uses a simile to tell us something about a boy named David. What do you think it is?

KINDS OF SIMILES

There are two kinds of similes. Similes with "as" tell us what the objects have in common. "My grandma is as slow as a turtle" is an example. We know for sure that your grandma and a turtle are both slow.

Similes with "like" are different. They take a little more work to understand. If you say, "My grandma is like a turtle," we don't know if you're talking about how slow your grandma is. You might actually mean she has wrinkly green skin! In these cases, readers use **context clues** to figure out the meaning.

Figure It Out

Use the context clues to help you figure out the meaning of the following simile: "Morgan's dad is like a giant! He's over six feet tall."

All About Context Clues

It's common to not understand everything you read. Good readers use clues to understand new ideas. Use the following tips and tricks to help you uncover their meanings.

✓ Look at the words before and after an unknown word or phrase. What do they tell you?

✓ Look for clues in the sentences that come before and after an unknown word or phrase.

✓ Look right after an unknown word or phrase. Is there a group of words closed off by commas? They may give you more information.

✓ Change an unknown word into a word you think means the same thing. Does it make sense?

ALL ABOUT METAPHORS

The comparison made by a metaphor is more powerful than one made by a simile. That's because a metaphor takes two objects that have something in common and makes them equal. It says an object *is* something else, not just *like* something else.

"A blanket of white snow covered the ground" is a metaphor. The metaphor tells you the snow covers the ground completely, in the same way a blanket covers a bed. This metaphor creates a very **vivid** picture, which helps keep your readers' attention.

Figure It Out

This sentence uses a metaphor to describe a girl named Gabriella. What does the metaphor tell you about her? "Gabriella is an angel," her mother said. "She always helps out with the chores!"

Look at the way the snow covers the ground. How does it remind you of a blanket on a bed?

15

COMMON PHRASES

Metaphors are everywhere. In fact, some of our most common phrases are metaphors. You've probably said them without realizing what they are! Have you ever heard the phrase "Life is a rollercoaster"? What about "Lily is a couch potato"? These metaphors create very vivid pictures. What pops into your mind when you read these metaphors?

Similes are just as common as metaphors. One very well-known simile is "Life is like a box of chocolates." Similes and metaphors become popular when they make comparisons many people find true.

Think about how the sun makes you feel, then think about how your friends make you feel. Do they have anything in common?

Figure It Out

"You are my sunshine" is a famous metaphor. What do you think it means?

BE LIKE SHAKESPEARE

Many familiar sayings come from books, plays, and poetry. William Shakespeare was a writer whose works are full of famous metaphors. Have you ever heard the phrase "All the world's a stage"? That comes from a Shakespeare play. It means people live out their lives much the same way actors perform parts in a play.

You don't have to be Shakespeare to include similes and metaphors in your own writing. A simile or metaphor can help you create a clear image in a reader's mind. It may even make them agree with your thoughts about something!

Figure It Out

Imagine you're reading an essay about summer school. The author says, "Summer school is a prison. We shouldn't have it anymore." What is the author trying to say?

18

WILLIAM SHAKESPEARE

Readers will enjoy your writing if you use similes and metaphors. It's a great way to make your point, while also being interesting!

19

WRITE YOUR OWN

Similes and metaphors can make your writing and speech more interesting and powerful. However, it's not always easy to come up with your own. Here are a few tips to get you started:

- Come up with something you want to describe.
- Think about the feeling or image you want to create.
- **Brainstorm** a list of things you can compare your object to.
- Share your ideas with someone to see if your point makes sense to them.
- Write!

If you follow these steps, you'll be comfortable using similes and metaphors in no time at all!

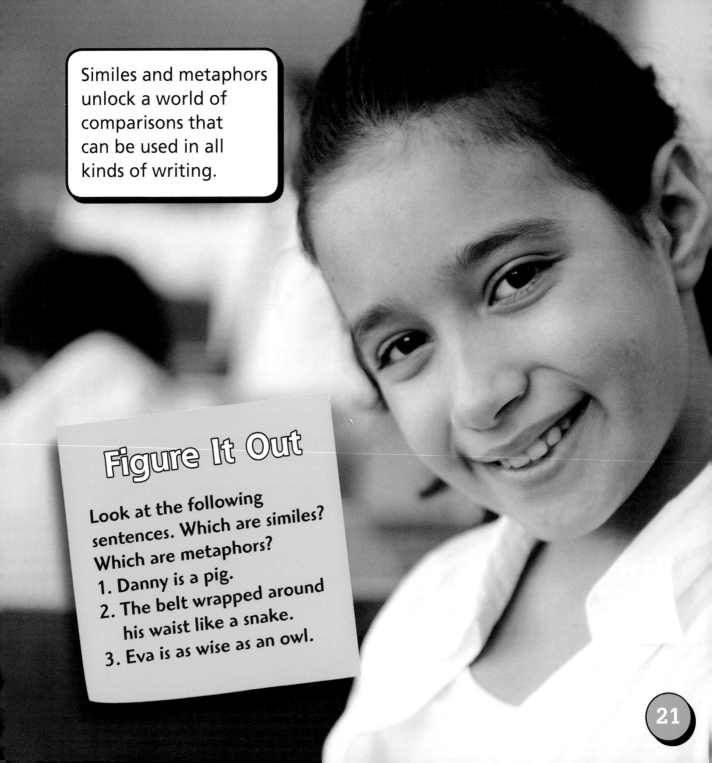

Similes and metaphors
unlock a world of
comparisons that
can be used in all
kinds of writing.

Figure It Out

Look at the following
sentences. Which are similes?
Which are metaphors?
1. Danny is a pig.
2. The belt wrapped around
   his waist like a snake.
3. Eva is as wise as an owl.

FIGURE IT OUT ANSWERS

Page 4: Similes use "like" or "as" to make a comparison, while metaphors don't.

Page 7: The hotel is probably big and pretty because palaces are big and pretty.

Page 8: It doesn't make sense because dragons usually aren't thought of as being happy.

Page 11: Oxen are known for their strength, so comparing David to an ox means he must be very strong.

Page 12: Most people picture giants as very tall. Since Morgan's dad is tall, he can be compared to a giant.

Page 14: People think of angels as being nice. Gabriella does all her chores, which is nice. That's why her mom compares her to an angel.

Page 17: Sunshine is bright, cheerful, and makes a lot of people happy. Comparing someone to sunshine says they are bright, cheerful, and make others happy, too!

Page 18: Prison is a bad place to be, and you don't have fun there. The author compares summer school to prison to say summer school is a bad place to be.

Page 21: 1. Metaphor 2. Simile 3. Simile

GLOSSARY

brainstorm (BRAYN-stohrm) To come up with ideas.

compare (kuhm-PEHR) To study two or more things in order to find what is the same and different about them.

context clue (KAHN-tehkts KLOO) A hint in a sentence that helps a reader figure out the meaning of a new word or idea.

describe (dih-SCRYB) To tell about something.

metaphor (MEH-tuh-fohr) A comparison that doesn't use "like" or "as."

simile (SIH-muh-lee) A comparison that uses "like" or "as."

vivid (VIH-vuhd) Producing strong, clear pictures in the mind.

INDEX

WEBSITES

Due to the changing nature of Internet links, PowerKids Press has developed an online list of websites related to the subject of this book. This site is updated regularly. Please use this link to access the list: www.powerkidslinks.com/cls/sime